P9-AFM-755

THE BUS
TO VERACRUZ

WITHDRAWN
UTSA LIBRARIES

WITHDRAWN
UTSA LIBRARIES

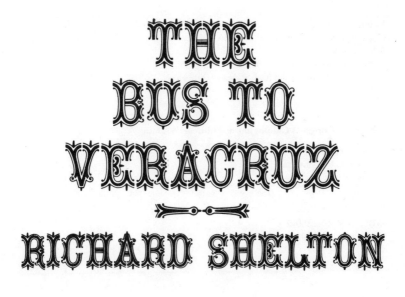

THE BUS TO VERACRUZ

RICHARD SHELTON

UNIVERSITY OF PITTSBURGH PRESS

LIBRARY
The University of Texas
At San Antonio

Published by the University of Pittsburgh Press, Pittsburgh, Pa. 15260

Copyright © 1978, Richard Shelton
All rights reserved

Feffer and Simons, Inc., London
Manufactured in the United States of America

Library of Congress Cataloging in Publication Data

Shelton, Richard, 1933–
    The bus to Veracruz.

    (Pitt poetry series)
    I. Title.
PS3569.H39367B8   811'.5'4   78-4168
    ISBN 0-8229-3380-2
    ISBN 0-8229-5296-3 pbk.

Acknowledgment is made to the following publications for permission to re-
print poems that appear in this book: *The American Poetry Review, Blue
Moon News, The Chowder Review, Glassworks, Grilled Flowers, Idaho Heri-
tage, The Iowa Review, Kayak, Madrona, Marilyn, The Mysterious Barricades*
(The Rainbow Press), *Nitty-Gritty, The Paris Review, The Salt Creek Reader,
Skywriting, South Shore* (Avery Color Studios), and *Westigan Review.*

"The Boojum Tree" and "The Bus to Veracruz" were first published in *The
Antioch Review*, vol. XXXIII, no. 1 (1975) and vol. XXXVI, no. 2 (1978)
respectively. "The Voice of the Moon," "Desert," and "Certain Choices" first
appeared in *Chosen Place*, by Richard Shelton, published by The Best Cellar
Press, 1975. The poems, "Five Lies About the Moon" (1975), "Mexico" (1976),
and "The Prophet" (1977), copyrighted © in the years shown by The New
Yorker Magazine, Inc. "The Blind" was first published in *The Ohio Review*,
vol. XIV, no. 2 (1973).

LIBRARY
The University of Texas
At San Antonio

*The publication of this book is supported by a grant
from the National Endowment for the Arts
in Washington, D.C., a Federal agency*

For Lois

CONTENTS

LANDSCAPE WITH A WOMAN

THE BOOJUM TREE

The dog days of a marriage have come
and gone for another year. What
is left of the raddled moon
stays up later than it did, and all
its complaints are legitimate.
The prickly pear is shriveled
from lack of water. Its fruit turns
from the color of new blood to the color
of old blood and drops away.

The worst is over. Through it all
the birds did not sing, but called
to one another: Are you there?
Are you there? And each afternoon
the clouds arrived on schedule,
bringing no rain.

During those days we learned
that the desert is not a metaphor.
I am punished for your sins,
and you are punished for mine.
Now the hideous boojum tree grows
upside down between us, an insane turnip.
We have learned not to trust
one another, never to trust anyone
who is dying of thirst.

THE SCHEDULE

Someone thinks of a secret
no longer worth keeping.
The sky darkens to rain.
You turn toward me with desire,
but it is not me you want.
It is yourself, the dream you are
never allowed to remember.

Someone's eyes flick
from the bottom of one page
to the top of the next. It is
morning. The date is not
a matter of choice. The weather
has been decided. I get out of bed
and put on my clothes. I light
a cigarette. I open a door
as if there were no tomorrow.
And there is no tomorrow.
There is only today.

TO MY OTHER SELF

when the warnings
have fallen into the wrong hands
never to be heard of again
and the Church of the Holy
Innocents is empty
we will meet where atheists
come to pray and believers
curse God and die

while the saw moves
and the wood says *thank you*
thank you thank you to its torturer
we will turn upon one another
with our knives dulled
in the service of banality

we will hear a snake gliding
through feathers and see
the hawk circling
with his eye on the sparrow
and we will know for one moment
exactly what is happening
and that it is happening to us

when the screams begin it will be
too late and when they cease
it will be much later
we will lie down together
and I will hold you hold you
in my bloody arms and each of us
will say to the other *I did it for you*
because I love you I did it for you

BALANCE POINT

there was never a better time to be going
nor a worse time to stay
yet we hesitate a little while
at the top of the mountain

on one side the desert
on the other a river and fields
was it just for the view we came so far

there are white flowers here
and one is being ridden shamelessly
by a yellow butterfly

a few clouds above us
tiny tongues in search of water
and the sun falling into a distant sea

it will be a long dark way
down whichever side of the mountain
we choose to go

either with knowledge
which is not sight not anything
but itself
or with wisdom in her ragged clothes
silent and waiting for the transformation

while the dead stars
keep sending their light
but from so far and to which interpreters

THE NEGATIVE VIRTUES

loneliness
is a luxury beyond the reach
of those who have no privacy left
and live in the hope
of its constant invasion
but to those
who have always been alone
it is a friend

poverty
gives us a sense of direction
when we don't know which way to go
and when we walk
on the edge of its cliff
we never go mad we can't afford to

fear
like courage and charity
begins at home and expands in circles
rocking all the boats it touches
and bringing in its wake
the last of the negative virtues

maturity
which is not what we wanted
but comes anyway when we realize
that the things we feared
as children
can no longer hurt us
and that we fear them no less

PAIN

the biggest bore in town
arrives at my party
as if he were invited

and begins to tell me
the details of what a terrible
time he had getting here

but it was worth it he says
and I know he will be
the last to leave

8

GUILT

you led me through cactus
all the way without shoes
leaving a trail wide enough
for anyone to follow
and the dogs with their noses
trained for blood

but if I hadn't known
where you lived
I couldn't have found you
here beyond the words
beyond the confession

guilt
among the strings
of whose harp I have blundered
as the crow flies
as the moon rises
expecting harmony to happen
by accident expecting
tired old men to emerge
from the village and say
we are glad you have come

and finding disgust
the perfect gift
the sweater you made for me
which does not fit but I will
wear it always
to please you

MY HANDS ARE MY ENEMIES

they want to caress
every beautiful face and body
we pass on the street

I conquer them I make them reach
for a doorknob pick up a pencil
open a book

but at night
when they take off my shoes
they tell each shoe
to wait for its lover in the dark

I have put my face into my hands
trying to forget it
but they reminded me
it was still the same face

I have picked up my name
like a frightened bird
and held it gently in my hands
begging them to let me keep
this fragile thing
as a pet
but my hands opened
and the bird flew away

I have trusted my scarred hands
but they have not been
faithful to me

and sometimes
when they think I am not looking
one of them takes
the other in its arms
whispering *hold me hold me*
what we wanted was always
beyond our reach
otherwise
we would not have wanted it

THE SWIMMERS

If we go back to the old places, we will be happy again. Let us run away to Mexico and live in the upstairs room of the house by the sea. It will be a second honeymoon. Do you remember the old house by the sea? The beach and the two young swimmers?

They have given us up, the young swimmers. They have left us behind. We did not love them enough; we did not cherish them enough. But sometimes at night they come to us through the snow, down the dirty side street, pale and shivering, a little drunk, carrying flowers. And we hear their laughter in the next room, like bells under water. We think they are happy, but later we hear them crying softly in the hall.

Let us go back to the house by the sea. From its tall windows we will look west across the Pacific. We will watch the young swimmers going out farther each day. One day they will not return. That night we will celebrate on the beach with fireworks, aiming our Roman candles at a point just above the horizon. One of our rockets will bloom like a giant hibiscus and fall slowly, petal by petal, into the open hands of the dead.

LANDSCAPE WITH A WOMAN

when shadows climb
out of the desert
up the sides of the mountains
and violent birds pass like projectiles
on their way home for the night
I say I have given you
everything it was all I had

when darkness rises
to the tops of the saguaros
and a river of cool air begins to flow
down the arroyo
I say I have given you
little it was all I had

when the moon
sits on top of the Santa Ritas
then levitates becoming smaller
and more pale as it goes
I say I have given you
nothing it was all I had

but you do not listen you go on
into your losses without birds
without mountains or shadows
or the moon you look into yourself
and say it is not enough
it was never enough

A BIRD IN THE HAND: TWO SOLOS

Wife: there was nothing wrong with our dreams
they fit us like scales on a fish

our dreams of patience and goodness
were not beyond our abilities
and our dreams of sex were harmless

there was nothing
wrong with our dreams except
they were the wrong dreams for us

now we see we had little choice
and once we had chosen each other
even that was taken away

Husband: when I reached out with my right hand
and touched you
I knew everything had been planned
even what I am saying now
had been prepared
for me to say

and if I had reached out
with my left hand
at a different time on a different day
you would have been there
and everything would be the same

Wife: coming of age
I found myself in the desert
following the wrong leader
but how could I have abandoned you
when I knew you would perish without me

14

so I said let it ride
and I rode with it
through a godforsaken land without trees
or flowers or anything beautiful
while the wind played my ribs like a harp

I don't enjoy being laughed at
but I have learned
to practice a certain amount of madness
most difficult of the arts
and the least rewarding

Husband: before we realized what they were
they were over
those days when we lived
in furnished rooms and could laugh
at their ugliness

later
well on our way
and established in our own shambles
drinking good wines and eating good salads
we gave up bread and butter
and those private days those brief
beautiful days

gladly
as if we had a choice

Wife: I keep busy all day
but when the sun goes down
I seem to go with it

once I walked out the door and entered night
because it was there
and because it promised everything
but what became of the promises
we didn't live up to

only the young are aware of life
burning at their shoulders
only they know his touch

later it is all speculation
and empty phone booths
waiting for violent acts of love

I keep telling myself I will
feel better tomorrow
but I don't believe it
there is always tomorrow night

Husband: I saw you sleeping
knees bent to the right a little apart
head turned to the left
right arm at your side and left arm
above your head with your hand
caught in the wildness of your hair

until I saw you like that
I never understood why
there were so many paintings of nudes

Wife: we are separate people
each what he fears most each his own
trap his own bait his own victim
I am not responsible for your life
and you are not responsible for mine

16

I wanted to get married
and you thought that meant I loved you

now you are going deaf and I pity you
how hard it must be for a man
who has been blind all these years

Husband: there are others
who had all the advantages I had
and kept them
but deafness grows
on my family tree like a vine
choosing one limb and avoiding another

now that my ears
have started to go blind
I find myself among the chosen
and someday I will hear the true sound
of darkness

I have learned to expose my eyes
to the lips of strangers
and understand what they cannot say

living as I do
with my secrets unheard
and listening always with my eyes
how can I blame you
if you turn your face away

Wife: all afternoon
your shadow your only child
grew taller

now he is leaving and you will be alone
in the darkness that has been
and the darkness that is coming
the same darkness

bright moons in the blood move on
as water moves in the bed of a river
sleeping at night and waking
somewhere else

once I turned quickly and saw you
looking only at me

even if I could explain I wouldn't
even if I could explain to you
I would oh I would

how any love story is a sad story
and we kiss ourselves goodby
each time we kiss each other

Husband: those who have no children
become the children they were
and those who have several children
extend themselves like fingers
stretching into deep grass

but we have only one child
and both of us must crowd into his body
elbowing each other for space

Wife: I remember
when this photograph was taken

18

the aperture opened on my life
as it was as it appeared to be
with the eyes of a deer on the wall
and a tongue which could tell
the truth
but the other was easier

my life created for me
and I like a fool accepted it
with its hand over its mouth
to hide the bleeding

waiting on the steps
of the front porch for years saying
you are young you will find somebody

my life with a life of its own
daring me to leave it
saying I am all I have it isn't enough

Husband: waiting is hardest but we have to wait
for the good things to come to us

I always have this next thing to do
while I am waiting
something important that needs to be done
a dog to be fed a plant to be watered

I had two friends
one is gone the other is dead
now our son is grown up and no longer
needs me and you say I am the cause
of all your unhappiness

these things are true
but there is always this next
thing to do something important
that needs to be done while I am waiting

Wife: ambition
worm in my bowels
the more I starve you the more you grow

others have killed their thousands
but you have killed your tens of thousands

I tell you
the stars can see only into the past
they do not know what I am doing
and do not care and the moon
which knows everything
cares even less

but you answer me with the story
about water always running away from home
and returning purified

Husband: years ago I took this woman
you took this man
and we kept each other
but each of us still wants to be a victim
as if love were an accident
caused by carelessness
and we could hold one another responsible

in order to get what we need from each other
what have we traded except parts of our lives
huge parts of our lives

and what have we gained
except huge parts of each other's lives
love always gives
more than we bargain for

Wife: I heard a bird cry a name
               and when I looked I found you
               in the trap of my hand
               crying a name I could not understand
               your own or the name of someone you lost
               it was never mine

               I tried to find someone to love me
               before it was too late
               but there was no one

Husband: I heard a bird call my name
               but when I found the bird
               it was you
               caught in the trap of my hand
               and what I heard was your pain
               it has always been

               I tried to find a place
               where I could not hear that sound
               but there was no place

Wife: *I heard a bird cry a name*
Husband: I heard a bird call my name
               and when I looked
                         it was you
               in the trap of my hand
                         what I heard was your pain

21

crying a name I could not understand
     it has always been
your own or the name of someone you lost
     it was never mine
I tried to find
     a place
someone to love me
     but there is no other place
there is no other one

ISLAND OF LIGHT

MEXICO

once each year
after a warm day in April
when darkness comes to the desert
uninvited but planning to spend the night
something hits me like a shovel
and I am stunned into believing
anything is possible

there is no overture to frenzy
I simply look up and see Scorpio
most dangerous of friends
with the last two stars in his tail
blinking like lights at a railroad crossing
while in one claw he holds the top
of a mountain in Mexico

and suddenly I know
everything I need is waiting for me
south of here in another country
and I have been walking through empty
rooms and talking to furniture

then I say to myself
why should I stay home and listen to Bach
such precision could have happened
to anyone to an infinite number
of monkeys with harpsichords

and next morning I start south
with my last chances flapping their wings
while birds of passage stream over me
in the opposite direction

I never find what I am looking for
and each time I return older
with my ugliness intact
but with the knowledge that if it isn't there
in the darkness under Scorpio
it isn't anywhere

THE LITTLE WIND WITHOUT A NAME

was born far from here
and wrapped in nothing
which she still wears

often at night I find her
as she moves down an arroyo
a light sound tiny fingers
on the door of a stone

we are two insomniacs
who encounter each other
late on an empty road
and walk together in silence

she with no language
and tormented by the desire
to speak and I with words
but afraid to say them

alone is a dark place where
whichever of its many faces
the moon turns toward us
is better than no moon at all

THE KINGDOM OF THE MOON

in the desert
it is not the sun
we get to know best
but the moon

we learn about it
when we are very young
and not a moment too soon

―――――

if you come here to stay
do not worry about
what will happen to you

the moon will take care of you
you will obey it
and the worst will happen

―――――

it is no use
asking the moon
philosophical questions

when it tells us anything
it tells us everything
always more
than we wanted to know

―――――

the moon commands the desert cold
a word so harsh
it splits the tongue
of the true aloe

the moon pulls stones
to the surface
and directs the ghosts
of dry rivers in their paths
toward the sea

the moon rules the wind
which will fall in love
with anyone
and run away but the moon
brings it back each time
without recriminations

———

at night my shadow
follows me through the desert
like a faithful snake

but it is not faithful to me
it is faithful to the moon

———

other moons
can be seen in other places
but the desert moon lives here
and it lives alone

its own friend its own company
its own comfort in the dark

THE VOICE OF THE MOON

When I wake in the night
troubled and thinking
I heard the cry of a bird,
I go to the window
and look out.

Then I realize
it was the cry of the moon.

———

Years ago I thought
I heard the voice of mountains
which spoke only at night.

Since then I have listened
many times, and I was mistaken.
It was the echo
of the voice of the moon.

———

When I am unhappy
the moon reminds me
that all things change.

When I am happy
it does the same thing.

———

I can believe that men
have walked on the moon.
Men would do a thing like that.
But when I am told the moon
is a huge round stone
which does not change its shape
and has no light of its own,
I cannot believe it.

I have heard the voice of the moon.

———

When I become confused
and do not know who I am,
I listen to the voice of the moon.

The moon knows who everyone is
and forgives all of us.

———

When the moon is new
it begins at the beginning
and tells the same story
straight through to the end.

It is a long story
but we listen and believe.
Who can doubt
the voice of the moon.

———

It is important
to learn the habits of the moon.

Otherwise, one might wait
all night and it would not appear.
And when the sun rose triumphant,
one might despair,
believing the moon had been
destroyed and would never return.

———

The sun is like fire.
It takes what it wants
and pays no attention to anyone.

But the moon knows each of us.
It looks into our eyes
and remembers all our names.

———

When we watch the sun go down
we are impressed with its glory.

When we watch the moon go down
we want to go with it.

———

The sea, the wind, and the owl
try to imitate
the voice of the moon,
but none succeed.

Beethoven and Debussy tried
to write its song, but compared
with the voice of the moon
one of them created the sound
of screen doors slamming,
and the other, the sound
of a pork chop being fried.

———

When the moon rises
in the afternoon and sets
too early to be of any use,
I remember how old I am
and that I no longer
have the option of dying young.

When I sleep and moonlight
comes through the window
and touches me,
I become a dream.

———

No man turns into a wolf
when the moon is full.

But wolves howl
when the moon is full
because they hear its voice.

———

Some think the moon is silent.

They are blind.

THE BLIND

we clench both our windows
tell us what you want the most
and we will tell you
in a dim voice
from behind the partition
why you won't get it

why you arrived too late
too early or at the wrong place
which was clear across town
so everybody was gone
when you got there

about the pool hustler
with a crippled arm
trying to make it one-handed
and the transvestite
trying to make it
in a land
which will never be home
the lack of choices

and out in the meadow
stumbling under a full moon
Lord what a light
has been given
to us who needed it least

CHILDREN OF NIGHT

I lay down
beside the body of the river
as if beside a beautiful woman
and all night she sobbed
that the light was gone
and would never return

at dawn a little wind
touched us gently
and when I woke she was singing
of the beauty of darkness

———

daylight arrives or departs
like royalty
with a fanfare of trumpets
and great banners in the sky

but darkness
sends no messengers before it
and arrives like water under the door
reminding us we are small and alone
and powerless to see

some of us accept it out of love
others out of fear
but none can send it away

———

when light is separated
into its parts
we see a rainbow
but darkness cannot be separated
darkness is all the same thing

when we enter darkness
we can no longer see where we are going
or where we have been
but we become more aware that we are

———

when the sun comes up
everything is waiting for it
but when the moon comes up
it is always a surprise

we malign the moon
when we say it is inconstant

the moon gathers whatever light
it can find in the darkness
and gives it all to us
keeping none for itself

———

when we enter darkness
we give up the light
but when we enter the light some of us
carry a little piece of darkness with us
and will not let it go
we are the children of night

DESERT

Sometimes the sun is still trying
to get to the horizon
when a daylight moon comes up,
fragile and almost transparent,
the ghost of a white bird
with damaged wings,
blown from its course and lost
in the huge desert sky.
It is the least protected
of all unprotected things.

A little wind goes by
through the greasewood,
heading home to its nest
among blue-veined stones
where it will circle three times
and curl up to sleep
before darkness falls
straight down
like a tile from the roof
of a tall building.

There are families of stones
under the ground.
As the young stones grow
they rise slowly like moons.
When they reach the surface
they are old and holy
and when they break open
they give off a rich odor,
each blooming once in the light
after centuries of waiting.

Those who have lived here longest
and know best
are least conspicuous.
The oldest mountains are lowest
and the scorpion sleeps all day
beneath a broken stone.

If I stay here long enough
I will learn the art of silence.
When I have given up words
I will have become what I have to say.

BURNING

I

each day comes here
to its own execution
to its own burning

at sunset the ashes
are sifted and scattered
until they are cool

then darkness walks barefoot
through the desert

II

today the rain kept
coming back as if it had
nowhere else to go

and each time
the desert welcomed it

the gates of the desert
never rust but they open
only to the voice of rain

III

even the Indians were
strangers in this place

our oasis is a mirage
and all day the desert
looks through us

at night it looks through us
and sees its own stars
its own moon burning

moon says its name
   as a sign in the sky
wind says its name
   which runs along behind it
   trying to catch up
road says its name
   as a casual promise
   and then moves on
mountain says its name
   in two languages both words
   are almost the same
bat says its name
   and listens for the echo
   which will guide it

coyote says its name
   again and again to the moon
   which pays no attention
palo verde says its name
   as a snare for the wind's name
   which runs along blindly
   trying to catch up
arroyo says its name
   to the coyote
   who translates it as home
place between two mountains
   says its name to the stars
   who say their names
   not quite in unison
owl says its name
   as a challenge to intruders
   who do not know the password
   is to repeat the name

40

darkness says its name
   which breaks into small pieces
   and hides from the moon
   in the arroyo
silence says its name
   softly the name of the place
   where it was born and lived
   until it died

THE NEW ROAD

I

Tonight at the end of a long
scar in the desert a bulldozer
sleeps with its mouth open
like a great yellow beast.

A coyote sits down to watch it
from a safe distance. An owl
questions again and again.
No answer. Someone is building

a new road, a fine road, wide
and smooth. The huge saguaros
in its path have stood here
two hundred years looking up

at the sky. This will be their
last chance to see the moon.
In the morning the yellow beast
will wake up and move toward them.

II

We believe in movement. We live
in the sanctity of mobile homes.
We are the children of those
who created the portable Indian

and moved him from place to place.
Ours is a republic of cylinders
and pistons, a republic of wheels.
Progress moves before us over

the hill and we pursue it as fast
as we can. With our horses
in trailers, our politicians
in limousines, and all our angels

on motorcycles, we pursue it.
The world rolls on and these gods
of the desert cannot get out
of its way. They are no use to use.

III

I have stroked them until my hands
are bloody, but what comfort
can I offer? They are doomed
and I am tired of being human,

tired of being mad in a mad world.
Now I lay me down in the new road
but to whom can I pray? The owl
has stopped calling. The coyote

gets up and fades away. I will
look at the moon as long as I can.
Then I will sleep in the desert,
helpless in the path of progress,
waiting for the sound of wheels.

THE PROPHET

recognized by the others
because his dog did not bark
identified and branded
citizen of neither country
he was banished and left behind
to guard the passes

where flowers dry
from natural causes and hang on
to be tormented by the wind
which goes by with some
destination in mind
but unsure of the right direction

and each morning
while stars flee for their lives
he remains and looks toward the east
knowing the sun would rise there
if it could

THE ANGEL AND THE ANCHORITE

For an angel went down at a certain season into the pool, and troubled the water: whosoever then first after the troubling of the water stepped in was made whole of whatsoever disease he had. —John 5:4

I

when the road forked
he took the middle way
and disappeared into the desert
but the pattern of the life he avoided
emerged as a birthmark on his hand

late one night he cut off the hand
carried it into a village
and left it
on the doorstep of the only house
with a light still burning

the note said *take care of my child*
it is an ugly thing
but I cannot bear to kill it

he hid at the edge of the road
and watched her open the door
he could not see her face
but in the light from the doorway
she seemed to be wearing a halo
as she knelt down quickly
taking his hand unwashed and bloody
into her slender arms

II

on the evening of the third day
when no miracle happened
he knew he would die soon

the road rose before him like a ladder
and he began to climb toward her
gripping each rung
with the only hand he had left

she found him outside her door
she touched his wound and said
this is where I was taken from
she put on his makeshift solitudes
and wore them like widow's weeds
she became the angel
who troubled his waters

III

each morning he rolls over
rising to the surface facedown
and she tries with all her strength
to revive him but he is lost
still wandering through the desert
hearing the stones' dry whispers

she watches him drift in his sleep
into another life
she cannot wake him
and she fears there will not be
enough of him left to love

when a white moon rises
with one edge frayed to nothing
an apparition for the dogs to bark at
darkness calls him like a prayer
he can hear but cannot answer

he feels the wind
blowing through that part of him
which is missing
he hears a lost child
crying for him and he calls out
here here I am but it passes him
stumbling through the desert nearby

he knows he must meet himself someday
under the only tree on the horizon
and he fears that meeting
more than he fears
thirst or the scorpion

IV

the stars point in all directions
and say *go quickly* but she circles
with one wing pinned to him

she no longer believes what he says
his lips are a perfect pair of liars
each verifying the other's
false story
but his hand is honest and has no ally

he says *do not love me*
I cannot carry your pain forever
he says *all we need to survive is patience*
and later we will need nothing

he sees the bridges
washed out between them and everywhere
but tomorrow arrives as if by water

47

V

they have lived together for twenty years
and they stand beside each other
almost transparent with suffering
they have become the color
of certain feathers
the color of one another

sometimes at night when the moon
rises full of hope and false information
and the acacia is juggling
thousands of tiny golden balls
they walk into the desert
knowing they will not go far
but they will go all the way together

at those times her eyes are luminous
with the fear of darkness
and of this desert place
which has never been her home

he takes one of her hands in his
and leads her into the night
he says *go carefully here my darling*
some of the stones are broken
but they are my friends

THE HEAVEN OF THE POOR

Blessed are the poor in spirit: for theirs is the kingdom of heaven.
—*Matthew* 5:3

I

through the needle's eye
we can see them
clamoring to get in
each offering to give up what he
cherishes most
not knowing he has become
what he cherishes most

we who are here
had nothing to give up
except our vanity and that
was not required
how can a weak man give up
his strength
or an ugly woman her beauty

in the heaven of the poor
the past keeps going away but is
never quite gone
I was young I was
so young I thought I would
get over it
and all I have learned
is that we never get over anything

some of us were born
to look for a child who has no legs
and wants only to dance
and when we find that child
we take it in our arms
like a flame
and dance and dance

II

among bricklayers and lawyers
and even poets there are
good people
who work alone
at honest and difficult professions
debauched by others

their reward
will be the heaven of the poor

when they see
the wormholes in the statues
and realize there are kings
who need no followers and have none
they will begin to escape
from the world

each of them will come to a river
and how he gets across it
if he gets across it
will be how he learns to swim

when he crawls out
wet and exhausted on this side
he will look back and see
the bridges he did not know he had
burning burning

III

there are no cities
in the heaven of the poor
no families no friends

we do not pray for what we want
nor do we pray for salvation
we have already
been saved and each night
our dreams show us what we wanted
and could never become

some of us walk on an empty beach
leaving no footprints
and others live
alone in the desert
accepting the rain as love

we do not call it happiness
exactly but we have the moon
to talk to and it always
answers us

do you believe me about the moon
do you think I care
whether or not you do

FIVE LIES ABOUT THE MOON

I. The Full Daytime Moon

She is a bald-headed woman. When someone
shouts "Fire!" she rushes from the building
without her wig. She becomes confused
in the crowd and turns down the wrong street.
We try not to look at her, pale and fragile
as a lost button in search of a shirt.

II. The Waning Crescent Moon

She is young and elegantly thin. She goes
to many parties but does not dance,
preferring to drape herself across a couch
where she is always surrounded by men.
Any of them would gladly place his neck
beneath her delicate foot. She is in love,
nobody knows with whom, and it is hopeless.
When she smiles sadly, they are overcome.
She goes home early and alone.

III. The Half-Moon

She loved her husband. The day he left her
for another woman, one side of her face
became paralyzed. Now she turns that side
away and faces the world bravely in profile.
It is unfair that she, of all women,
should have a Roman nose and a weak chin.

IV. The Gibbous Moon

She has lost both her money and her figure
and is defenseless, wearing secondhand light.
Still, she does the best she can to keep up
appearances, and goes from place to place
as she did in the past. Often when she
arrives at the proper address,
perspiring and late, nobody is home.

V. The Full Harvest Moon

She wears gold carelessly, because it is
expected, but she glows from within. Although
she has pressing duties to perform, she moves
through the crowd in the palace hall as if
there were no hurry. The men gasp at her beauty
and the women turn pale with chagrin. Without
slowing her progress toward the door, she offers
a sincere word and a special look to each of them.

THE POET AS EQUESTRIAN

Be a man with calm eyes who laughs,
who silently laughs under the calm wing of his eyebrow . . .
—St.-John Perse, translated by Louise Varèse

with the pale horse
under your right foot
the dark horse under your left
keeping your balance astride
two beautiful animals
between which is death
horseman ride on
past all the places you have ever been

past your childhood's house
with nobody home
where the furniture settled for good
the plumbing died the roof fell in
and the walls and ghosts
hold one another in the rain
horseman ride on
like a leaf from the calendar
torn off by the wind

past your friends
the con men who call you brother
and tell you the secret of the world
a different secret each time
but will desert you
far from the promised land
when you have nothing to carry with you
and nothing to leave behind
still believing them
horseman ride on
where you go you will go alone

chosen to survive when you were young
you traded the cow for a sack of beans
and learned to climb
you found the golden harp
that sang the music in your head
you listened to the stones and understood
their darkness and stayed awake
all night waiting
for the resurrection of the light

you will outlive your gifts
and even then horseman ride on
the good do not live forever
and the bad live only a little longer
horseman be stronger and when the crowd
wants entertainment
entertain
take down the harp
from where it hangs and make
its tinny strings the victims
of your ruined hands

for you it will be the long way home
you will never find your way now
to the heaven of the brilliant
lucky poets who die young
and when those who praised you
turn away one by one
ride on ride on
with nothing in your eyes but sadness
and the sun

THE BUS TO VERACRUZ

The mail is slow here. If I died, I wouldn't find out about it for a long time. Perhaps I am dead already. At any rate, I am living in the wrong tense of a foreign language and have almost no verbs and only a few nouns to prove I exist. When I need a word, I fumble among the nouns and find one, but so many are similar in size and color. I am apt to come up with *caballo* instead of *caballero,* or *carne* instead of *casa.* When that happens, I become confused and drop the words. They roll across the tile floor in all directions. Then I get down on my hands and knees and crawl through a forest of legs, reaching under tables and chairs to retrieve them. But I am no longer embarrassed about crawling around on the floor in public places. I have come to realize that I am invisible most of the time and have been since I crossed the border.

All the floors are tile. All the tiles are mottled with the same disquieting pattern in one of three muddy colors — shades of yellow, purple, or green. They make me think of dried vomit, desiccated liver, and scum on a pond. The floor of my room is dried vomit with a border of scum on a pond, and like most of the floors it has several tiles missing, which is a great blessing to me. These lacunae are oases in the desert where I can rest my eyes. The nausea from which I suffer so much of the time is not caused by the food or water, but by the floors. I know this because when I sit in the town square, which is covered with concrete of no particular color, the nausea subsides.

The town is small, although larger than it would seem to a visitor — if there were any visitors — and remote. It has no landing field for even small planes, and the nearest railroad is almost one hundred kilometers to the east. The only bus goes to Veracruz. Often I stop at the bus terminal to ask about the bus to Veracruz. The floor of the bus terminal is scum on a pond with a border of desiccated liver, but there are many tiles missing. The terminal is always deserted except for Rafael and Esteban, sometimes sitting on the bench inside, sometimes lounging just outside the door. They are young, barefoot, and incredibly handsome. I buy them *Cocas* from the machine, and we have learned to communicate in our fashion. When I am with them, I am glad to be invisible, glad that they never look directly at me. I could not bear the soft velvet and vulnerability of those magnificent eyes.

"When does the bus leave for Veracruz?" I ask them. I have practiced this many times and am sure I have the right tense. But the words rise to the ceiling, burst, and fall as confetti around us. A few pieces catch in their dark hair and reflect the light like jewels. Rafael rubs his foot on the floor. Esteban stares out the filthy window. Are they sad, I wonder, because they believe there is no bus to Veracruz or because they don't know when it leaves?

"Is there a bus to Veracruz?" Suddenly they are happy again. Their hands fly like vivacious birds. "*¡Sí, hay! ¡Por supuesto, Señor! ¡Es verdad!*" They believe, truly, in the bus to Veracruz. Again I ask them when it leaves. Silence and sadness. Rafael studies one of the tiles on the floor as if it contains the answer. Esteban turns back to the window. I buy them *Cocas* from the machine and go away.

Once a week I stop at the post office to get my mail from the ancient woman in the metal cage, and each week I receive one letter. Actually, the letters are not mine, and the ancient woman has probably known this for a long time, but we never speak of it and she continues to hand me the letters, smiling and nodding in her coquettish way, eager to please me. Her hair is braided with colored ribbons, and her large silver earrings jingle when she bobs her head, which she does with great enthusiasm when I appear. I could not estimate how old she is. Perhaps even she has forgotten. But she must have been a great beauty at one time. Now she sits all day in the metal cage in the post office, a friendly apparition whose bright red lipstick is all the more startling because she has no teeth.

The first time I entered the post office, it was merely on an impulse to please her. I was expecting no mail, since no one knew where I was. But each time I passed, I had seen her through the window, seated in her metal cage with no customers to break the monotony. She always smiled and nodded at me through the window, eager for any diversion. Finally one day I went in on the pretext of calling for my mail, although I knew there would be none. To avoid the confusion which my accent always causes, I wrote my name on a slip of paper and presented it to her. Her tiny hands darted among the pigeonholes, and to my astonishment she presented me with a letter which was addressed to me in care of general delivery. She was so delighted with her success that I simply took the letter and went away, unwilling to disillusion her.

As soon as I opened the letter, the mystery was solved. My name is fairly common. The letter was intended for someone else with the same name. It was written on blue paper, in flawless Palmer Method script, and signed by a woman. It was undated and there was no return address. But it was in English, and I read it shamelessly, savoring each phrase. I rationalized by convincing myself that the mail was so slow the man to whom the letter had been written was probably already dead and could not object to my reading his mail. But I knew before I finished the letter that I would return to the post office later on the chance there might be others. She loved him. She thought he was still alive.

Since then I have received one letter each week, to the enormous delight of my ancient friend in the post office. I take the letters home and steam them open, careful to leave no marks on the delicate paper. They are always from the same woman, and I feel by now that I know her. Sometimes I dream about her, as if she were someone I knew in the past. She is blond and slender, no longer young but far from old. I can see her long, graceful fingers holding the pen as she writes, and sometimes she reaches up to brush a strand of hair away from her face. Even that slight gesture has the eloquence of a blessing.

58

When I have read each letter until I can remember it word for word, I reseal it. Then, after dark, I take it back to the post office by a circuitous route, avoiding anyone who might be on the street at that hour. The post office is always open, but the metal cage is closed and the ancient one is gone for the night. I drop the letter into the dead-letter box and hurry away.

At first I had no curiosity about what happened to the letters after they left my hands. Then I began to wonder if they were destroyed or sent to some central office where, in an attempt to locate the sender and return them, someone might discover that they had been opened. Still later, the idea that some nameless official in a distant city might be reading them became almost unbearable to me. It was more and more difficult to remember that they were not my letters. I could not bear to think of anyone else reading her words, sensing her hesitations and tenderness. At last I decided to find out.

It took months of work, but with practice I became clever at concealing myself in shadowy doorways and watching. I have learned that once each week a nondescript man carrying a canvas bag enters the post office through the back door, just as the ancient woman is closing her metal cage for the night. She empties the contents of the dead-letter box into his canvas bag, and he leaves by the door he came in. The man then begins a devious journey which continues long into the night. Many nights I have lost him and have had to begin again the following week. He doubles back through alleys and down obscure streets. Several times he enters deserted buildings by one door and emerges from another. He crosses the cemetery and goes through the Cathedral.

But finally he arrives at his destination — the bus terminal. And there, concealed behind huge doors which can be raised to the ceiling, is the bus to Veracruz. The man places his canvas bag in the luggage compartment, slams the metal cover with a great echoing clang, and goes away.

59

And later, at some unspecified hour, the bus to Veracruz rolls silently out of the terminal, a luxury liner leaving port with all its windows blazing. It has three yellow lights above the windshield and three gold stars along each side. The seats are red velvet and there are gold tassels between the windows. The dashboard is draped with brocade in the richest shades of yellow, purple, and green; and on this altar is a statue of the Virgin, blond and shimmering. Her slender fingers are extended to bless all those who ride the bus to Veracruz, but the only passenger is an ancient woman with silver earrings who sits by the window, nodding and smiling to the empty seats around her. There are two drivers, who take turns during the long journey. They are young and incredibly handsome, with eyes as soft as the wings of certain luminous brown moths.

The bus moves through sleeping streets without making a sound. When it gets to the highway, it turns toward Veracruz and gathers speed. Then nothing can stop it: not the rain, nor the washed-out bridges, nor the sharp mountain curves, nor the people who stand by the road to flag it down.

I believe in the bus to Veracruz. And someday, when I am too tired to struggle any longer with the verbs and nouns, when the ugliness and tedium of this place overcome me, I will be on it. I will board the bus with my ticket in my hand. The doors of the terminal will rise to the ceiling, and we will move out through the darkness, gathering speed, like a great island of light.

REACHING FOR THE GUN

THE MESSENGER

There was no question of waiting for daylight, and I had expected the cold, but not the creaking as some unseen engine hoisted a damaged moon into the sky. Then I saw molting angels, like scarecrows, standing in the fields while their feathers blew in drifts across the road. But none of this could stop me. I had memorized the message. I had sworn to deliver it. And it would prevent an execution scheduled for dawn.

When I arrived at the gates of the city, they were closed for the night. I beat on them with my fists. Pigeons rose with a clatter of wings and circled above, but nobody came to open the gates. So I searched for crevices between the stones and began to climb the wall. The fear of heights rode my back like a terrified child with its arms too tight on my throat, but at last I reached the top of the wall and descended into the city, my message secure and my fingers bleeding.

Then I ran down dark streets, slippery where night jars had been emptied, and past barred windows behind which the rich and poor lay dreaming. I envied them their sleep. And as I passed one doorway, I smelled sickness and heard someone call out. It seemed like my name. But I ran on with each breath burning deeper in my chest. I told myself to keep going, keep going, you must do this one thing.

And I found the place, almost by instinct. It was in the center of the city, a large public building, ancient and formidable, with a courtyard where a crowd had gathered around a fire. I went straight to the fire, and the people made room for me. I could see their faces. From time to time they looked up at one lighted window above, and at those times their eyes were as dim as lanterns in distant trees.

But just as I was beginning to feel the warmth of the fire, a fat guard came up and demanded my papers. I told him I didn't have any. Then he asked for my name. In my fear and confusion I told him I didn't have a name either. He laughed, slapping his huge

63

belly, and as he walked away, still laughing, the shield hanging on his back reflected light on the crowd around me. They were laughing too, and their faces were strange and contorted. But above their laughter I could hear another sound. It was as familiar as the squeal of a rusty hinge or the cry of an infant, but I could not identify it. It might have been a wolf howling on the slopes outside the city, or a woman in labor in one of the neighboring houses. I could not tell.

A man in the crowd stared at me with hard eyes and asked if I had come to give evidence at the trial. I told him I was a stranger in the city, that I had stopped to warm myself by the fire on a cold night, that I didn't know anything about it. Then a servant girl came to the lighted window and emptied a basin of water which ran over the stones of the courtyard, and everyone scrambled to avoid it. In the firelight it looked like blood. And I heard the sound again. Perhaps a whip descending or the cry of someone in pain.

Then a woman approached me, smiling. Her teeth were rotten; her breath stank of old wine. She made secret signs, offering me her body, and she led me to an aisle where the horses were tethered. When she undressed, her body was ugly; but I lay with her to prove I could observe the customs of the city. And as we got up from the dirty straw, I heard the sound again. This time I was sure it was a human voice, and I asked the woman if she knew who had cried out. But she looked at me strangely and said it was only the cock crowing to warn us of approaching dawn. Then we returned to the fire, and I saw shadows moving behind the lighted window as if a procession were passing from the room, down a stairway lit by torches, and out into the earliest light of morning. But I remained in the courtyard with the other messengers.

We warm our hands at the fire and salvage what comfort we can from dawn and the news of distant disasters. We have heard rumors of cataclysms, of storms, and of the darkening sun in other places. But we have been here for years, and the road no longer remembers the sound of our feet. Each morning we return from sleep as if from a long journey, forgetting the messages we have memorized and sworn to deliver in our dreams. Forgetting even our dreams, the unspeakable solutions to problems we no longer have.

REACHING FOR THE GUN

superficial among the superficial
I have come home
it's a crowded neighborhood
and I go over the long list
of things I don't believe in
as if it mattered on this street
what I do or do not believe

the drunks next door
are beating their child again
taking turns at it
I hear screams
and a thud as the child's knees
hit the floor did that hurt
did that does anything

turning away so I cannot
see through the window
I tell myself I don't
believe in people
but I know I believe in pain

the ultimate goodness
the only goodness which lasts
is the ability to forgive
and I don't have it

I don't believe in murder I say
reaching for the gun and wondering
if Hell is where we wake up dead
and realize how much life
we had left that we didn't use

LINES

At dusk a man takes down the flag and begins to fold it.
The stars are the last things to disappear.
In each of his fingernails a moon is rising.

A woman is removing her makeup.
She breaks her mirror and deep lines form on her face.
All night her shoes have an orgy on the closet floor.

At dawn a yellow bulldozer attacks a field of wild flowers.
A hunter yawns in the early light and raises his rifle.
The fillings in his teeth shine like newborn children.

The woman picks up her mirror and folds it.
Her shoes are wild flowers on the closet floor.
In each of her teeth a moon is breaking.

The man begins to raise his flag among the children.
The stars bloom like tiny broken mirrors.
Deep fields of rifles yawn in an orgy of light.

All day the hunter moves through lines of wild flowers.
His yellow fingernails shine like deep mirrors.
The moons are the last things to disappear.

At dusk the woman removes her face like makeup.
The fillings in her teeth yawn in the mirrors.
A broken moon begins to rise from her closet floor.

All night the hunter gives birth to shining rifles.
A bulldozer attacks the folded children.
At dawn it fills deep lines with tiny faces.
The broken shoes are the last things to disappear.

DEATH ROW

have you been to the land of carnivorous birds
where brown leaves hang on all winter
rattling for release and the fences are strands
of blood strung between living scarecrows

a flat land of small farms
where those who cannot afford a river
build their houses beside a dry ditch
and live behind fever's old walls
while the curtains burn at every window
and outside the dogs bark all night

where each tree waits for its rope
while the stars fall away toward morning
and months come out of the future like bullets
striking the last leg of a one-legged
journey the last arm raised
to shield the last pair of eyes

have you been to that land did you
stumble upon it as a tourist how long
did you stay and can you hear them
calling you still can you hear them calling

CERTAIN CHOICES

My friend, who was a heroin addict,
is dead and buried beneath trash
and broken bottles in a prison field.

He died, of course, because of the way
he lived. It wasn't a very good way,
but it kept him alive. When it couldn't
keep him alive any longer, it killed him.
Thoroughly and with great suffering.

After he had made certain choices,
there were no others available. That's
the way it is with certain choices,
and we are faced with them so young.

I have few friends, and none of them
are replaceable. That's the way it is
with friends. We make certain choices.

THE TOWER

the prisoners in the tower of justice
have tiny feet like mice
and when someone calls
Rapunzel Rapunzel
they run to their little high windows
but they have no hair

the hidden prisoners without noses
hang in their cages in the tower of justice
and the wind blows over the wall
bringing to their little high windows
the odors of mesquite and acacia
after rain

if they had eyes
the prisoners in the hidden tower of justice
could see the edge of the moon
one night each year
from their little high windows
and if they had tongues they could speak
for the unseen and unforgiven

or the prisoners
in the tower of hidden justice
could signal from their little high windows
with their hands
but their hands have been taken from them
and now the windows are no longer needed
so they are taken also

and the prisoners
fold their arms without hands
and remain silent and hidden in the dark
tower of justice
and remain and remain

MY OTHER FRIENDS

I go to the State Prison once a week.
We sit in a circle and confess our sins.
The prisoners are appalled at mine.
My sin is fear. I built this place,
I tell them, and I put you here.

One by one they take my hand and tell me
it is never too late to change.
They will help me. They will comfort
me when the old nightmare returns.

Next day, my other friends tell me
I should stay home: Prisons are best
kept out of mind and I would not go there
if I had ever been the victim of a crime.

But I know the victims of crime.
I have just come from them. So I tell
my other friends as best I can
to go to Hell. I go there once a week
and each week a different part of me
never comes home again.

HARRY ORCHARD

You lived out of town where the land
sloped up to Table Rock. The prison
looked exactly as a prison should,
except for the roses in front: walls
of granite blocks held together
by their own weight and our fear.
We didn't know what went on in there;
we didn't want to know. The river
kept running. Summer brought heat,
winter brought snow. The grounds
outside the prison were always neat
and the roses were magnificent.

Because of you I grew up thinking prisons
were places outside towns where men
who had the knack for it retired
to tend their roses. I was a child
when I first heard your name, and I
thought you had always been an old man
with a cane who came out and knelt down
stiffly, like in church, among the flowers.
And I thought, because you were so good
at growing things, they named an avenue
in our town, *Orchard,* after you.

When you and the state were young
you were convicted of placing a bomb
on the Governor's gate. He came home
and opened it; it was the last gate
he ever opened. There had been a fight
between miners and the owners of the mines.
You were labor. The Governor was on the side
of management. It's strange how times
and governors don't seem to change.

I don't know whether or not you did it;
but I can imagine you hiding among the vines
which covered the wall outside his mansion,
young and terrified, with sticks of dynamite
like a bouquet in your hands. That was
the picture the state's lawyers painted,
but there were questions about who hired you,
questions about two union bosses and a lawyer.
Somebody paid to shut those questions up.

And what did you do? Oh, Harry! Harry!
You know what you did. You got religion
in the county jail, and when they brought
you to the trial, forgave them all: forgave
the union bosses and the owners of the mines,
forgave the State Militia for their guns,
forgave the men who built the bullpen
at Coeur d'Alene, forgave the striking miners
who starved in it, forgave the Governor,
forgave the crooked lawyers, forgave everyone.
You took it on yourself and praised the Lord,
and even Clarence Darrow couldn't help you then.

Harry Orchard, you lived in prison so long
that when they offered you a pardon in old age,
you refused it. By then you couldn't give
that garden up. And I believe what rumor
later said about the prisoners whose bodies
disappeared after they were beat to death
or died from lack of care, how they were buried
by guards after dark in a place no one would
suspect or dare to desecrate. How many
left their cells to feed the flowers?

And I see you still. It is late afternoon.
You are kneeling in a flower bed, a trowel
in your hand, while all your roses flame.

We always build our prisons out of town
so we won't have to look at them. But we
saw yours. Whole families of us drove
out there to see your roses bloom. We also
saw the statue of the Governor, downtown
in front of the State Capitol, its head
and shoulders white with pigeon droppings.
It's still there, on a traffic island.
Only tourists look at it, and never more
than once. At its base some scraggly roses
grow with yellow leaves and hardly any bloom.
Some things even the state can't do.

Harry Orchard, there stands the Governor
with an iron jaw, squat and menacing,
the ugliest thing a schoolboy ever saw.
Somebody blew him up and he went
straight into the history book we
had to read, but we could never remember
his name. Harry Orchard, we remember
yours because for over fifty years
outside the gates of Hell you grew
the most beautiful roses in all Idaho.
When you died, you went straight into fame.

ONE MAN'S MEAT

1956: She is the girl with the biggest
breasts in Sloan, Iowa. She will take
a backseat to no one. He is young
and handsome. All summer he fondles
her breasts in the front seat. Sometimes
she rests her fingers on the round knob

of the gearshift. *1957:* After the wedding
they live in a white house. She suspects
he is colorless. One day, while she
is shopping, he paints the house green.

She says it is garish. *1960:* She decides
he lacks polish. For his birthday she
gives him sandpaper. He uses it, hoping
to please her. When his face bleeds,
she says he lacks character. He drinks
to ease the pain. She says he is going
to the dogs. To avoid it, he drinks alone.

1963: His face has healed but is scarred.
She says he is hideous; he should take
care of himself. She suggests a diet,
exercise, vitamins. He prefers alcohol,

loneliness, pain. *1965:* She tells him
he neglects her. She threatens to take
a lover. The next day he brings home
a friend. She and the friend become lovers.
After three months the friend kills
her and goes to the mountains of Peru.
The husband is convicted of murder and goes
to prison, where he is almost happy.

1975: But the mountains of Peru are very
high. The friend has a heart attack
and dies. Before he dies, he confesses
to the murder. The husband is released

from prison. *1976:* His hair is beginning
to gray, but in spite of the scars he is
still handsome. He takes a job
driving a truck and meets a waitress
in a truck stop. She is a grass widow
with the biggest breasts in Enid, Oklahoma.
She will take a backseat to no one.

THE STAR

he was born into a traveling
troupe of dramatists performing
a tragedy and told he would
someday be a great star

he took care of the props
kept the dagger in a box
with velvet lining and filled
the vial of poison with colored

water each night but the show
lost money it became a romance
he dusted the artificial roses
combed the wigs the reviews

were bad it moved to a remote
area and became a melodrama
he cleaned the long black cape
painted freckles on the heroine

it was booed off the stage
and became burlesque he sewed
sequins on the G-strings
kept the bladder in good repair

the sheriff ran it out of town
it became a circus but the tent
blew down before his trapeze
act it was made into a movie

with his part cut when the film
was edited now he drinks and watches
reruns on television waiting
to see his face hear his voice

but the life he never appeared in
is the only show in town

THE LAST TIME

Schmid, 32, died Sunday in a Phoenix hospital from wounds suffered in an attack in a trusty dormitory at the prison March 20. Dr. Heinz Karnitzchnig, Maricopa County medical examiner, said his autopsy found 47 stab wounds in Schmid's body. He said the most destructive wounds were in a lung and a kidney.

—Tucson Daily Citizen, April 5, 1975

I should never have listened. I should
have left you alone in that place.
Dark as it was, it was not as dark
as the place you are now. I wanted
you to be good, but I did not tell you
the good are vulnerable, that no slate
is ever wiped completely clean.

I wanted you to be able to love,
to be able to trust. It took years,
but you learned so well you could trust
anybody. Even me with my platitudes.
Even them with their can openers.

They must have wanted you to die slowly;
they stabbed you so many times and never
touched your heart. We who care most,
who are most ruthless, go for the heart.

When you thanked me for letting you
into my world, I should have known
you could not survive in that world
without your cunning, without your fear.
And when you said I had made you feel
almost beautiful, I should have foreseen
blood on the floor, blood on the ceiling.

You were not beautiful when I saw you
the last time, blind and butchered,
trapped in a web of tubes and machines,
unable to speak, unable to do anything
but listen to my words, my lies, my evasions
which dripped into you as if through tubes.
You were my perfect captive audience,
and whose world were you fighting for then?

Oh Paul, when you come back,
as I know you will, with the white rose
of the grave on your shoulder, do not
come to me, please do not come to me.
I have no more help to give, no further
instructions. I am guilty. And I
could not bear to see you that way again.

SOFTLY SOFTLY

for Paul David Ashley

I

one day in April
when the palo verdes
have become golden beehives
and the acacia is showing
some promise of green
summer arrives in Sonora
full-grown
without remorse
without consulting anybody

on that day
the arms of the ocotillo
bend toward the earth
and at the end of each arm
is a hand filled with blood

every year in the desert
spring dies suddenly
while it is still young
and foolish and beautiful
and I survive

II

death is a poor child
without a mother or father
how could I turn him away

and once I have taken him
into my arms
and cared for him
I will not be afraid of him
when he returns as a man
still needing me
and calling my name

III

where the sky is king
no tree grows very tall
and flowers
the colors of dawn and sunset
bloom and fade quickly

when there are no second chances
there is no regret
only sadness
which surrounds us
and carpets our steps
like luxury

those of us who know
we will never come back
from wherever we are going
see the beauty
of the landscape
through which we pass

and when it is too late
life begins again
softly my friend
softly

ENCOUNTER

In some small flatland town
a stranger waits for me to arrive by train
and when I step down not knowing
where I am or why I have come
I will recognize him and give him my hand
He will fold my pain like a newspaper
and tuck it under his arm
He will take charge of everything

He will open a car door
I will get in and he will drive
expertly down Main Street out of town
toward open country where the sky
is half the world

As night comes on
we will hear grass beside the road
whispering of its native land
and when the stars bear down like music
I will begin to understand how things
that have never happened before
can happen again

PITT POETRY SERIES

Ed Ochester, General Editor